KING'S DECREE

CALEB BRUNDIDGE

SPRING HUEMME

King's Decree

Copyright © 2015 – Caleb Brundidge and Spring Huemme

djcaleb1@me.com

Calebbrundidge.com

decree *[dih-kree]*

a formal and authoritative order, especially one having the force of law

a judicial decision or order

one of the eternal purposes of God, by which events are foreordained

TABLE OF CONTENTS

KING'S DECREE

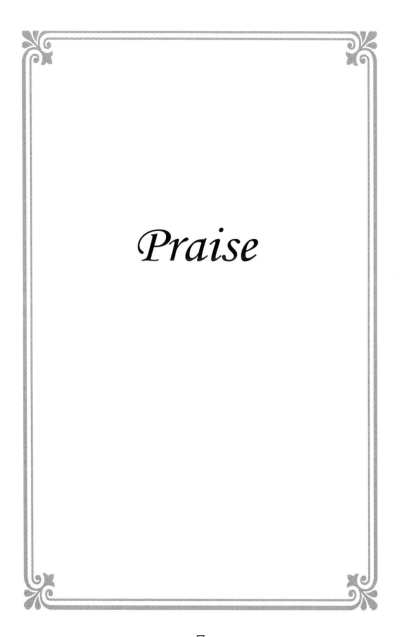

Praise

KING'S DECREE

I decree and declare, Jesus, that:

♦ You are King

♦ You are good

♦ You are mighty

♦ You sit on the throne forever

♦ You live forever

♦ You are righteous

♦ Your love is unfailing

♦ You are strong

♦ Your love is everlasting

♦ You are great, robed in majesty

♦ You placed the world on its foundation

♦ You fill the earth with the fruit of Your labor

- You are the Resurrection Power
- You are great and greatly to be praised
- You are the Creator
- You are creativity
- You are my Rock, my Fortress
- You are faithful
- You care about me
- You are trustworthy
- You protect me
- You are my Joy
- You are my Hiding Place
- You surround me with songs of victory
- You surround me with songs of praise

- ◆ Your heart is pure

- ◆ You spoke and the heavens were created

- ◆ You are a Priest forever

- ◆ Your work is great

- ◆ Your work is honorable

- ◆ Your work is wonderful

- ◆ Your praise endures forever

- ◆ You are the Light

- ◆ You are the Way

- ◆ You are the Truth

- ◆ You are the Promise

- ◆ You are my Friend

- ◆ You are my Brother

- ♦ You are my Father

- ♦ You are my Husband

- ♦ You are my Confidante

- ♦ You are my Heart's Desire

- ♦ You are the air that I breathe

- ♦ You are the Way-Maker

- ♦ You are the Bright and Morning Star

- ♦ You are color

- ♦ You are my Daily Bread

- ♦ You are my Joy in the morning

- ♦ You are my Song

- ♦ You are my Warring King

- ♦ You are my Lover

- ♦ You are strong

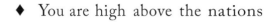

PRAISE

- ♦ You are high above the nations

- ♦ You are my Help

- ♦ You are my Shield

- ♦ You are worthy

- ♦ You are Love

- ♦ You are increase

- ♦ You are awesome

- ♦ You are brilliant

- ♦ You are always aware of me

- ♦ You are interesting

- ♦ You are magnificent

- ♦ You are Royalty

- ♦ You are the Lion of Judah and cannot be tamed

- ◆ You are my Peace

- ◆ You hold my future in Your hands

- ◆ You are my Everything

- ◆ You are my Banner of Victory

- ◆ You are my Healer

- ◆ You are my Deliverer

- ◆ You are my Redeemer

- ◆ You are my Provider

- ◆ You are the Lifter of my head

- ◆ You are the King of Glory

A awesome, amazing, apostolic, affectionate, aware, accurate, appealing, Alpha and Omega

B beautiful, believing, beckoning, bountiful, benevolent, breakthrough, bold, beginning and the end

C creative, courageous, colorful, capable, covering, capturing, clever, consuming, caring, calculating, compassionate, Chief Cornerstone

D delightful, delivering, drastic, detrimental, decisive, dangerous, diverse, deliverer

E epic, exceptional, extravagant, equipping, evangelistic, exciting, everlasting

F friendly, fundamental, flavor, forgiving, family, finishing, firm foundation

G giving, good, gigantic, generous, great, gentle, God all by Yourself

H huge, hilarious, healing, high, hovering, hoping, help in my time of trouble

I Irresistible, intimate, inspirational, indescribable, Immanuel

J just, Jehovah, jubilant, Jesus

K kind, keeping, King of Kings

L loving, living, luxurious, listening, Lover of my soul

M marvelous, magnificent, moving, mysterious, Master of all

N noble, neat, notorious, numbering, nice

O   open, official, omniscient, offering, omnipresent

P   present, pastoring, preaching, providing, Prince of Peace

Q   quiet, questioning, quantum

R   restoring, resting, repositioning, royal, reputable, reconciling, real, redeemer

S   strategic, supreme, saving, supernatural, sending, Shepherd

T   terrific, tremendous, training, tangible, Teacher

U   unique, unveiling, unusual, understanding, unbeatable, unfailing, undeniable, unshakeable

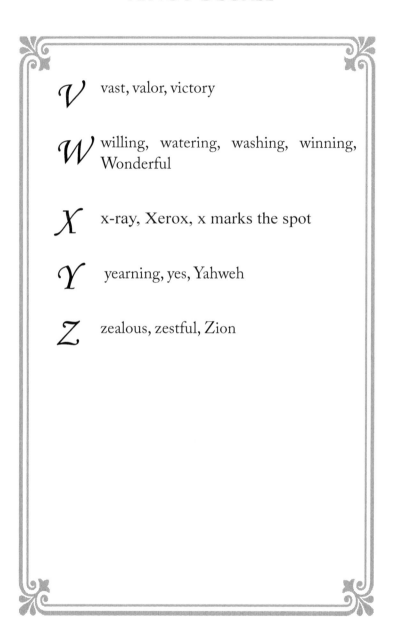

V   vast, valor, victory

W   willing, watering, washing, winning, Wonderful

X   x-ray, Xerox, x marks the spot

Y   yearning, yes, Yahweh

Z   zealous, zestful, Zion

Creating Atmospheres

KING'S DECREE

I decree and declare by the power of the Blood of Jesus that:

- This is the day that the Lord has made, I will rejoice and be glad in it.

- Today is good and perfect because every good and perfect gift comes from God.

- Today is pregnant with purpose, promise and potential.

- Today brings divine opportunities that I discern and take full advantage of.

- God has granted me strategies for a prosperous and successful life.

- My mind is filled with the knowledge of my true identity.

- I am becoming all that I was born to be.

- ♦ My life is in sync with the perfect will of God. My life reflects God's glory.

- ♦ My family and friends are blessed with all good things.

- ♦ My relationships are healthy, motivation is solid, and vision is clear.

- ♦ My prayers, praise and giving are forever increasing.

I decree and declare by the power of the Blood of Jesus that:

♦ My life is characterized by the fruit of the Spirit.

♦ My access to the gifts of the Spirit is unlimited. God pours out His unmerited favor on me.

♦ I walk in righteousness, honor, humility and holiness.

♦ I am a mover and shaker, a history-maker.

♦ I am a speaker of truth.

♦ I make a difference in the lives of others and in this world.

♦ My good name goes before me.

♦ God blesses the works of my hands.

- ♦ All I create, invent, and produce are in high demand.

- ♦ Excellence is the signature upon all I do and say.

- ♦ I think big and outside of the box.

- ♦ Every good seed I plant yields a fruitful harvest.

I decree and declare by the power of the Blood of Jesus that:

♦ My mind is clear and my thoughts are clear. My ears are always filled with good news.

♦ My mouth is full of His praise.

♦ My hands are full of productive and prosperous work.

♦ My mind is overflowing with million-dollar ideas and billion-dollar inventions.

♦ My spirit is filled with God's peace and presence.

♦ My soul is overflowing with joy and gratitude.

♦ My words build others up.

♦ My feet are forever moving forward.

- ◆ My heart is full of courage.

- ◆ My every action and activity is in sync with Heaven's rhythm.

- ◆ My home is full of music and laughter.

- ◆ My children fulfill their purpose and maximize their potential.

I decree and declare by the power of the Blood of Jesus that:

- I never settle for less than I deserve.

- I expect only the best for my life.

- I am happy with who I am and what I am called to do.

- I am a wise decision maker.

- My blessings are too numerous to count.

- My victories are as abundant as the grains of sand. Health and wealth walk with me hand-in-hand.

- God has granted me multiple streams of income.

- I navigate these streams with business savvy.

◆ My income is always greater than my expenditures. I am resourceful.

◆ I am a giver and always have more than enough to give.

◆ There is no lack in my home. My bank accounts are filled.

◆ My network and influence continue to increase daily.

Angels

KING'S DECREE

♦ I am the righteousness of God and angels have been sent to minister to me. They respond to the Word of God, which I speak. Therefore, as I speak forth the Word of God, I loose angels on assignment.

♦ I say today, let the Lord be magnified, who takes pleasure in my prosperity.

♦ In the name of Jesus, I command the angels to bring to me prosperity in my spirit, in my home, in my body, in my family life, in my finances and in all that pertains to me.

♦ I declare promotion, and command the angels to bring promotion into my life.

♦ I have a blood-bought covenant pro-mise from God Almighty to multiply exceedingly.

- I command the angels of God to go and bring this covenant to pass in my life now!

- I confess I am exceedingly fruitful and blessed.

- I have the power to obtain wealth, and I release the angels to bring wealth into my life.

- I declare right now that I am healthy, healed, delivered, and freed from the bondage of sin.

- I am the head always and never the tail. I am above only and never beneath.

- I lend, not borrow, and everything I put my hands to prospers.

- I walk in the favor of God and my favor is increased even as I am speaking.

- ♦ I have more than enough money to pay every bill that comes in, and I declare that I am totally debt-free now!

- ♦ I have the authority of Heaven and in the name of Jesus, I declare that whatever I bind on the Earth, is bound in Heaven, and whatever I loose on the Earth, is loosed in Heaven.

- ♦ I am free from unforgiveness and I set my will to forgive anybody for anything, no matter what!

- ♦ I walk in the love of God toward everyone, no exceptions!

- ♦ I send my angels forth right now to do God's pleasure and bring these words to pass. Angels, go now, and minister prosperity unto me, in Jesus' name!

KING'S DECREE

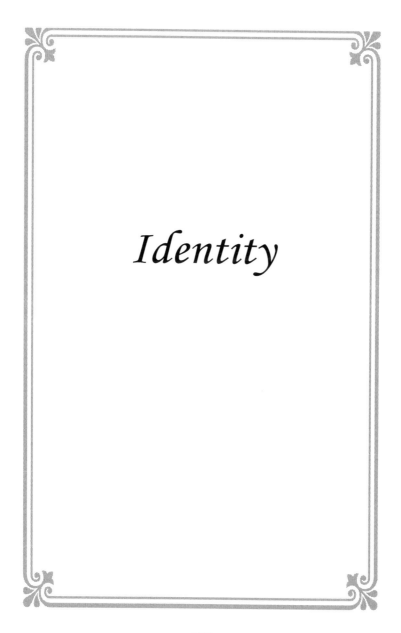

Identity

I decree and declare by the power of the Blood of Jesus that:

- ♦ I am made in the image of God

- ♦ I am marked by majesty

- ♦ I am fashioned and formed by divinity

- ♦ I am a creative, spiritual & powerful being

- ♦ I am a force to be reckoned with

- ♦ I am incredibly special

- ♦ I am undeniably unique

- ♦ I am fearfully and wonderfully made

- ♦ I am created for greatness

- ♦ I am brilliant

- ♦ I am gorgeous

- I am talented

- I am fabulous

- I am a child of God

I decree and declare by the power of the Blood of Jesus that:

- ♦ I was created to shine and to shine brightly

- ♦ I was born to manifest the glory of God

- ♦ I am a man/woman of integrity

- ♦ I am a speaker of truth

- ♦ I am courageous

- ♦ Courage is my constant companion

- ♦ I choose to live authentically

- ♦ I maximize my potential

- ♦ I reside in a wealthy place

- ♦ I am a lifetime learner

- ♦ I am resourceful

- ♦ I am victorious

- ♦ I bear fruit – fruit that remains

- ♦ I am more than a conqueror

- ♦ I live for God

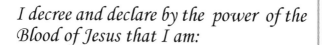

I decree and declare by the power of the Blood of Jesus that I am:

♦ A new creature in Christ

♦ Fearfully and wonderfully made

♦ Saved by grace

♦ Forgiven

♦ Redeemed

♦ Beloved of God

♦ Seated in Heavenly places

♦ A royal priesthood, a chosen generation

♦ The light of the world

♦ Free from condemnation

♦ Set free

♦ Significant

- Victorious

- Complete in Him

I decree and declare by the power of the Blood of Jesus that:

- I operate in excellence

- I am a trailblazer

- I break through glass ceilings

- I choose love

- I take calculated risks

- I am strong

- I have godly character

- I am prosperous

- I am generous

- I am blessed with all good things

- I am a good friend

- ♦ I make a difference in this world

- ♦ I am making an impact on my generation

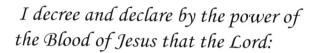

I decree and declare by the power of the Blood of Jesus that the Lord:

♦ Calls me His own

♦ Is faithful

♦ Establishes me

♦ Guards me from the evil one

♦ Is with me

♦ Guides me with His eye

♦ Is my strength

♦ Is my help

♦ Is my shield and buckler

♦ Upholds me with His righteous hand

♦ Is my refuge and fortress

- Began a good work in me and is faithful to complete it

- Orders my steps

- Shows Himself strong on my behalf

- Abides in me, and I in Him

- Makes all grace abound toward me

- Is the King

- Strengthens my heart

I decree and declare by the power of the Blood of Jesus that I:

- ♦ Am His

- ♦ Am hidden safely in His hand

- ♦ Am strong and of good courage

- ♦ Am chosen

- ♦ Am royalty

- ♦ Am holy

- ♦ Am special

- ♦ Am a King's kid

- ♦ Am a new creation

- ♦ Am strengthened in faith

- ♦ Am loved

I decree and declare by the power of the Blood of Jesus that:

- ◆ Daily I seek God and find Him
- ◆ God's kindness does not depart from me
- ◆ My light shines before men
- ◆ I have favor with God and man
- ◆ I live in peace
- ◆ I abide in His love
- ◆ I have abundance for every good work
- ◆ I wait upon the Lord and renew my strength
- ◆ I run and don't grow weary
- ◆ My hope is in the Lord
- ◆ God's Word is hidden in my heart

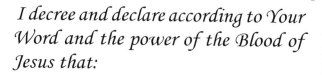

I decree and declare according to Your Word and the power of the Blood of Jesus that:

♦ I am a king and priest, washed by Your blood.

♦ My mind is stayed on You — every thought exalting itself is taken captive — all of my thoughts and meditations are on You.

♦ My mouth is anointed with kindness and my words are filled with grace and life; they build up all those that hear them.

♦ I live, move and have my being in You. You alone are the reason that I move and breathe and have my being.

♦ I am seated in Heavenly places with an ear to hear the conversations of Heaven.

I decree and declare according to Your Word and the power of the Blood of Jesus that:

♦ My gates of praise give You entrance — I am open to You, King of Glory.

♦ I draw from the deep wells of salvation, taking hold of all healing and deliverance that dwell within.

♦ My heart is in Your hand and You are the Master Potter, molding me into a vessel of honor and praise.

♦ My thoughts are not of this world as You have captivated my heart.

♦ I stand in a large place with a straight and smooth road before me.

♦ My steps have been ordered since before the beginning of time.

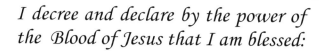

I decree and declare by the power of the Blood of Jesus that I am blessed:

◆ To be a blessing

◆ When I come and when I go

◆ To bear fruit and fruit that remains

◆ With all spiritual blessings

◆ In daily provision

◆ In my finances

◆ In my emotions

◆ In the marketplace

◆ In my relationships

◆ In my communications

◆ In my health

- ♦ Spiritually
- ♦ With victory
- ♦ Complete in Him

Father, You have given me the power to make wealth for Kingdom purposes. Therefore, I decree and declare that the supernatural abilities, gifts and talents that You have created in me will come forth in abundance.

In the name of Jesus I decree according to Your Word:

♦ Abundance replaces lack

♦ What the locust has eaten, You are restoring

♦ The work of my hands is blessed

♦ Creative ideas are continually birthed in and through me

♦ Witty inventions are being crafted

♦ Heaven on earth in my finances

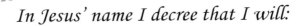

In Jesus' name I decree that I will:

- Be faithful with what You provide for me

- Give thanks for Your provision

- Deal honestly with everyone

- Praise Your name continually

Father, You said that Your Word will accomplish what You sent it forth to do and that it will prosper in that assignment. You have also said that Your Word is truth and that the truth will set me free. Therefore, I declare that Your Word goes before me to destroy the plans of the enemy set against me.

I decree and declare in the name of Jesus that Your Word:

♦ Shatters strongholds in my life

♦ Lights my path in dark places

♦ Positions me for success

♦ Gives me boldness and courage

♦ Brings life in place of death

♦ Ushers in Heaven on earth

In Jesus' name I decree that I will continue to:

♦ Listen to Your voice

♦ Heed Your Word

♦ Boldly step out in faith

♦ Declare Your plan in my life

About the Authors

 *Spring Huemme*

Spring Huemme is the Executive Administrator for His House in Oceanside, CA and Personal Assistant to Caleb Brundidge. She has a heart for the nations and is passionate about partnering with others to bring forth the Kingdom of God. With a nonstop thirst for prayer and a compassion for the lost, she will not be silent until all have an opportunity to call upon His name! With the prophetic gifting, Spring will draw you in to the Father's presence with sincere worship. Spring truly believes that Truth received by one is Truth revealed globally.

Caleb Brundidge

Caleb Brundidge travels worldwide as God's *Standard Bearer* releasing His praises in and through the earth. He has been an itinerant minister with Patricia King and the XP Ministries team for over six years. Caleb is a sought after minister in and outside of the church, revealing a deeper dimension of the Lord in all he does; flags, prayer, intercession, preaching, teaching, praise, and DJ style worship. He is passionate about an intimate relationship with Jesus, out of which flows a lifestyle of ministering the Kingdom of God around him. It is common for God encounters, miracles, salvations, and life transformations to take place as he ministers.

www.calebbrundidge.com

KING'S DECREE